The Spanish Conquest of the Americas

Diana Ferraro

Series Editor **Rob Waring**

Level 3 - ❷

The Spanish Conquest of the Americas

Diana Ferraro

© 2017 Seed Learning, Inc.

Series Editor: Rob Waring
Acquisitions Editor: Liana Robinson
Copy Editor: Casey Malarcher
Cover/Interior Design: Andy Roh

ISBN: 978-1-9464-5220-7

10 9 8 7 6 5 4 3 2 1
21 20 19 18 17

Contents

Europeans and Their Needs

Five hundred years ago, Europeans dreamed of a better life. They ate well, but they wanted to eat better. They wanted pepper and other spices. Spices came from Asia by land, and they were very expensive.

Christopher Columbus

A famous sailor, Christopher Columbus, thought he could reach Asia faster by sailing west. The queen and the king of Spain accepted his plan. They paid for the ships he needed and his travel. Columbus set off west to Asia.

Columbus explains his project to Queen Isabella and King Ferdinand.

4

Asians and the Land East of Them

Between Europe and Asia and between the Pacific and the Atlantic Oceans, there is a large and long land.

When Columbus sailed, no one in Europe or Asia knew about this land or the people who lived there.

The Asians didn't remember that thousands of years ago, some of them had gone to this new land.

Petroglyphs in California

Cave paintings in the Cueva de las Manos, Patagonia, Argentina

The People in the New Land

In this new land, some cultures had remained very simple, but others had developed.

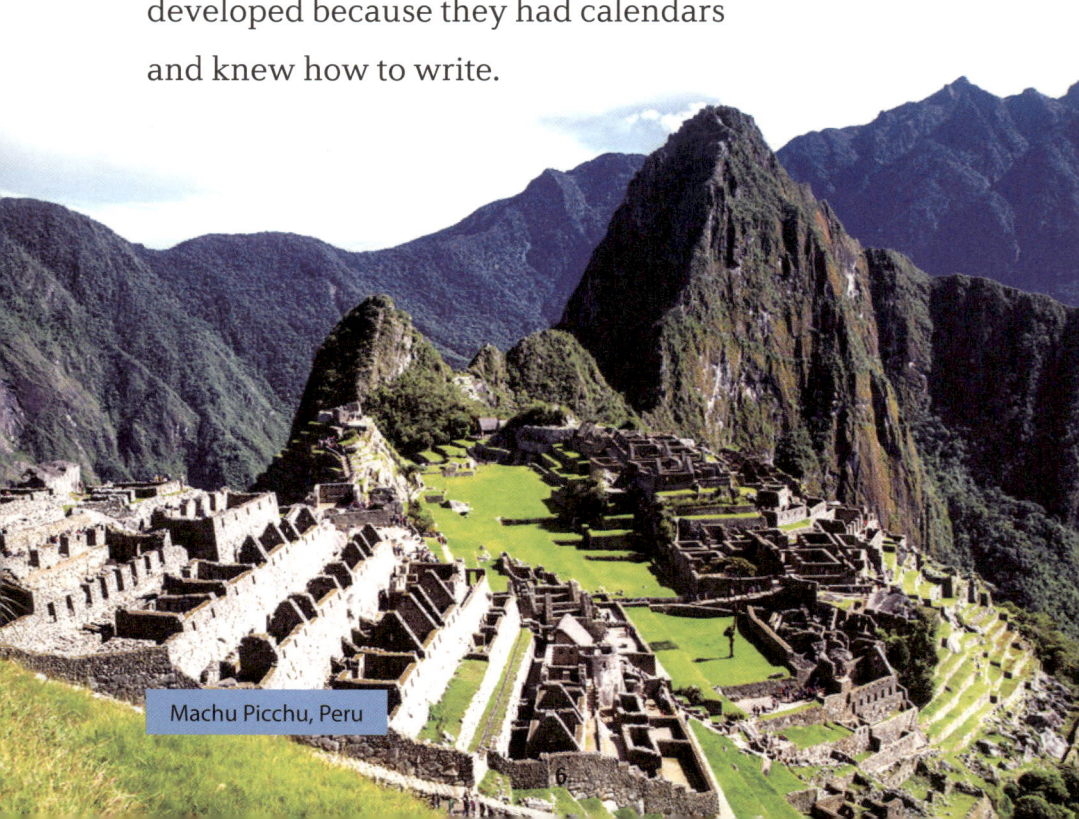

Aztec calendar

By the time Columbus sailed, the most important cultures were the Aztecs, the Mayas, and the Incas. Their cultures were quite developed because they had calendars and knew how to write.

Machu Picchu, Peru

6

The wall of an Ancient Mayan Tomb

These cultures built pyramids and big cities. They believed in different gods. They used silver and gold. They knew how to fight their enemies.

In addition, there were different groups of people with very simple cultures. They often fought each other for land or food.

A Mayan Pyramid at Chichen Itza, Mexico

Aztec Pyramids at Teotihuacan, Mexico

7

Christopher Columbus

Columbus sailed with his three ships. He traveled for 36 days. When he landed on one small island, he thought he was in India! He called the people "Indians."

Columbus went back to Spain but later made three more trips. On his last trip, he found the mainland.

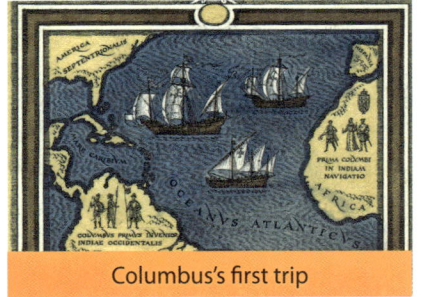
Columbus's first trip

When he died, he still didn't know how far Asia was or how big the new land between Europe and Asia was.

Columbus's first view of the New World

Amerigo Vespucci

The New World was called America by Amerigo Vespucci. Vespucci was another explorer who traveled along the coast of South America. He was the first one to understand he was not in

Discovery of the American Continent by Amerigo Vespucci

Asia but in a new land. He named it after himself and so it became the Americas.

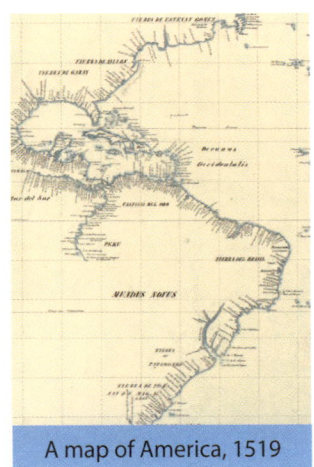

A map of America, 1519

A statue of Amerigo Vespucci

More Than Just Spices

The Spaniards were excited with the new land they had discovered. The explorers had different interests. Some wanted to become rich, others wanted to spread their religion, and yet others were simply interested in making more discoveries. The queen and king of Spain wanted silver and gold.

A conquistador—a Spanish soldier

Thousands of Spaniards sailed to the Americas, hoping to get what they wanted.

A conquistador with the Spanish flag

Explorers and Conquerors

The Spanish explorers wanted to go as far as possible and find new lands. Nothing stopped them. They soon explored the Americas from Florida to Argentina.

A Mayan king

Conquistadors like Hernán Cortés and Francisco Pizarro didn't want to explore. They wanted to conquer the land and own it. They wanted money and gold for themselves and their king. They fought until they won.

Francisco Pizarro draws a line to divide the land.

Cortés and the Aztecs

Hernán Cortés

When Hernán Cortés arrived in Mexico, he met Montezuma, the king of the Aztecs. Because the Aztecs believed the god Quetzalcoatl would return one day, Montezuma believed the Spaniards were gods. All was peaceful for a while.

Later, other Spaniards arrived who wanted to replace Cortés. At the same time, some natives rebelled. A war began and Montezuma died.

Many Aztec people died from smallpox—a disease the conquistadors introduced. Those remaining fought against Cortés. Even though Cortés only had 600 soldiers, he defeated the Aztecs.

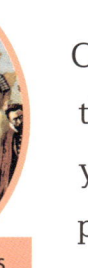

Hernán Cortés destroys his ships to prevent escape by his unhappy followers.

Cortés began a new government in the name of Spain. One hundred years after the conquest, the Aztec population had decreased from 25,000,000 to 1,000,000.

Pizarro and the Incas

Meanwhile, Francisco Pizarro heard about the Inca's gold and silver in Peru. Excited by the success of Cortés, Pizarro attacked the Incan Empire. He killed Atahualpa, the king of the Incas. Pizarro entered the capital city, and soon the Incan Empire belonged to Spain.

The execution of Atahualpa

What Spain Brought to America

The Spanish brought horses, cows, sheep, pigs, chickens, big dogs, and cats to the Americas. They also brought guns, cannons, a new religion, and plants such as wheat and rice.

The Spanish brought horses and many other animals to the New World.

Not everything that they brought was a benefit for the Americas. The Spaniards also brought diseases that killed the native people.

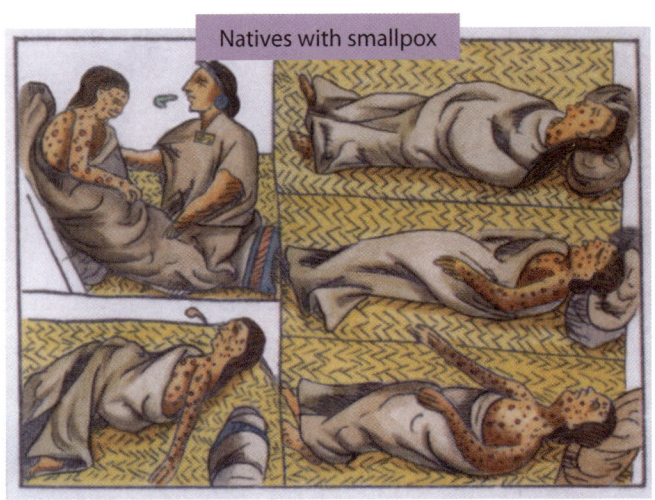

Natives with smallpox

What America Gave to Europe

America gave Europe many new goods, too.
Among them were potatoes, corn,
tomatoes, chocolate, vanilla, tobacco,
turkeys, bell peppers, avocados, and
pineapples.

Potatoes

Corn

Vanilla

Chocolate

Owners and Workers

The Battle of Otumba

In the Americas, the Spaniards planted cities and took control of the land. The native people were forced to work for the Spaniards. They were not paid, and they were poorly fed. They felt a great resentment toward the Spaniards. By the end of the 16th century, Spain ruled the Americas.

Cortéz and some native people in Mexico

Life After the Conquest

After the Spanish conquest, the Americas changed. People spoke Spanish. They became Catholics and lived according to the Spanish culture and laws. The cities looked like cities in Spain. For three centuries, what is now Hispanic America was ruled by Spain.

A church in Cuenca, Ecuador

From the time of Columbus, other European countries wanted to settle in the Americas, too. They conquered and won other parts of the new land, such as the British in North America.

In the 19th century, the Hispanic countries fought for their independence from Spain. They became independent republics. However, we can still see Spain's influence in their language, culture, and beliefs.

Hispanic America

Comprehension Questions

1. The Spaniards began conquering the Americas…
   - (a) 10 centuries ago
   - (b) 5 centuries ago
   - (c) 2 centuries ago
   - (d) 1 century ago

2. What did Columbus want?
   - (a) To discover America
   - (b) To buy chocolate
   - (c) To reach Asia
   - (d) To find gold

3. Who lived in the Americas before the Spaniards?
   - (a) No one
   - (b) Europeans
   - (c) Africans
   - (d) The Aztecs, Mayas, and Incas

4. The first inhabitants of the Americas were called "Indians" because…
   - (a) that is what they called themselves.
   - (b) they looked like Asians.
   - (c) Columbus thought he was in India.
   - (d) they came from India.

5. The New World was named…
   - (a) after Vespucci.
   - (b) after Columbus.
   - (c) after Cortés.
   - (d) after Pizarro.

6. Cortés and Pizarro did NOT want to explore to…
   - (a) conquer the land.
   - (b) find gold.
   - (c) be kings.
   - (d) find riches.

7. Who destroyed the Incas?
   - (a) Columbus
   - (b) Vespucci
   - (c) The Aztecs
   - (d) Pizarro

8. What did Spain bring to the Americas?
   - (a) Potatoes
   - (b) Rice
   - (c) Tobacco
   - (d) Avocados

9. Which is NOT true about the natives under Spanish rule?
   - (a) The natives were not paid to work for the Spaniards.
   - (b) The natives were hungry.
   - (c) The natives went to Africa.
   - (d) The natives were angry.

10. What happened to the native people after the Spanish conquest?
    - (a) They spoke English.
    - (b) They became Catholics.
    - (c) They defeated the British.
    - (d) They became richer.

Key 1. (b) 2. (c) 3. (d) 4. (c) 5. (a) 6. (d) 7. (d) 8. (b) 9. (c) 10. (b)

Glossary

- **Aztec** a member of the American Indian people who lived in Mexico
- **belief** a strong feeling that something is true or real
- **conquer** to take control of a country or defeat people in war
- **conquest** the act of taking control of a country or area
- **conquistador** a conqueror; one of the Spanish soldiers in the conquest of the Americas
- **disease** an illness
- **explorer** someone who travels to places where no one has ever been
- **Hispanic America** the region of the Spanish-speaking nations in the Americas; Spanish America
- **Inca** a member of the South American Indian people who lived in the Andes
- **independence** freedom from outside control or support
- **Mayas** a member of the American Indian people who lived in Guatemala and Mexico
- **rebel** to fight against a person in power
- **republic** a country that is governed by an elected leader (such as a president) rather than by a king or queen
- **resentment** a feeling of anger about an unfair situation
- **smallpox** a disease that causes fever, spots on the skin, and often death
- **Spaniard** a Spanish person
- **spice** a substance used to give a special taste to food

Image Credit/Pages

World History Timeline

This chart shows a rough overview of world history.
Some of the dates have been simplified.

World History Timeline

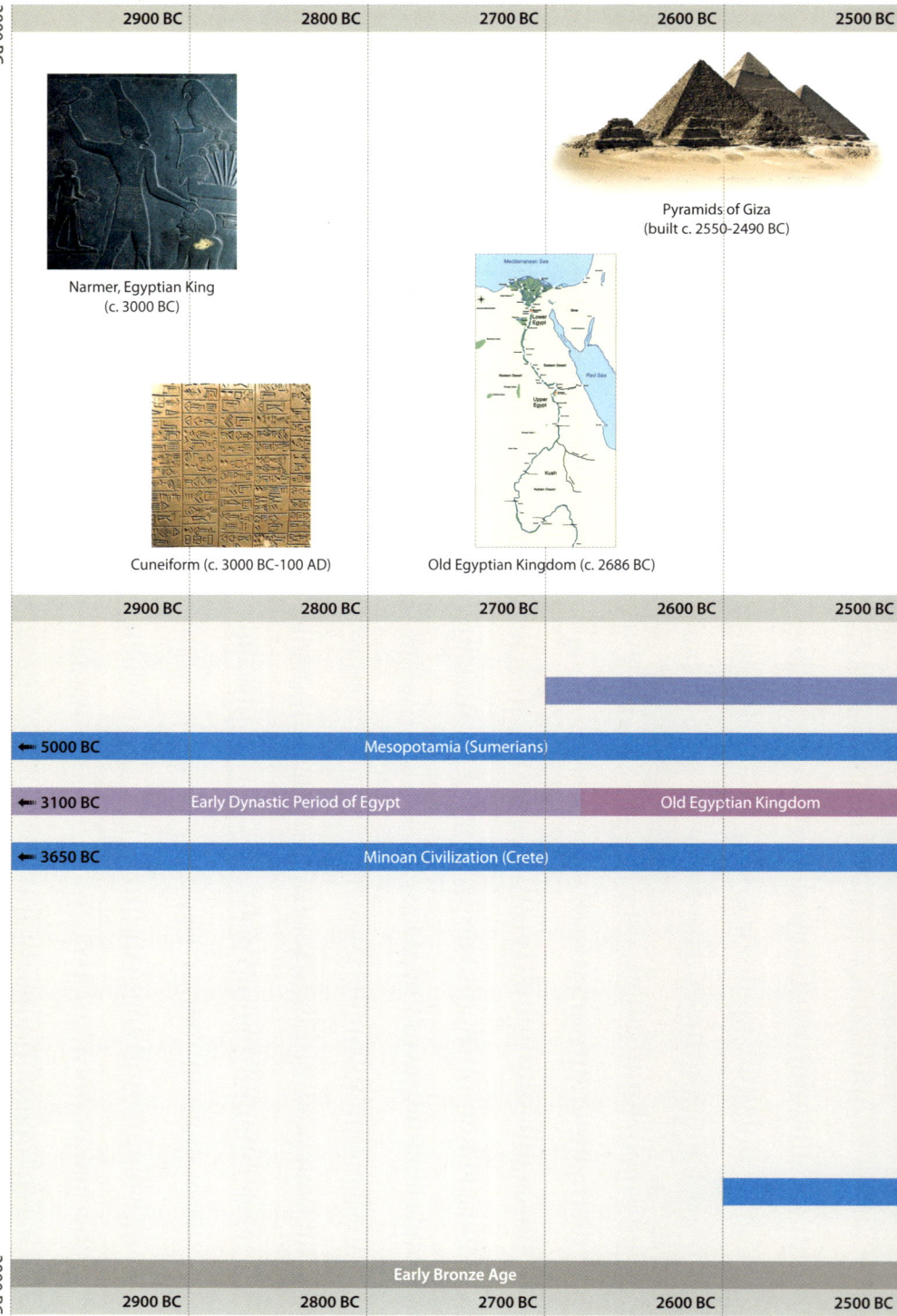

3000 BC	2900 BC	2800 BC	2700 BC	2600 BC	2500 BC

Narmer, Egyptian King
(c. 3000 BC)

Pyramids of Giza
(built c. 2550-2490 BC)

Cuneiform (c. 3000 BC-100 AD)

Old Egyptian Kingdom (c. 2686 BC)

2900 BC	2800 BC	2700 BC	2600 BC	2500 BC

← 5000 BC Mesopotamia (Sumerians)

← 3100 BC Early Dynastic Period of Egypt   Old Egyptian Kingdom

← 3650 BC Minoan Civilization (Crete)

Early Bronze Age

3000 BC	2900 BC	2800 BC	2700 BC	2600 BC	2500 BC

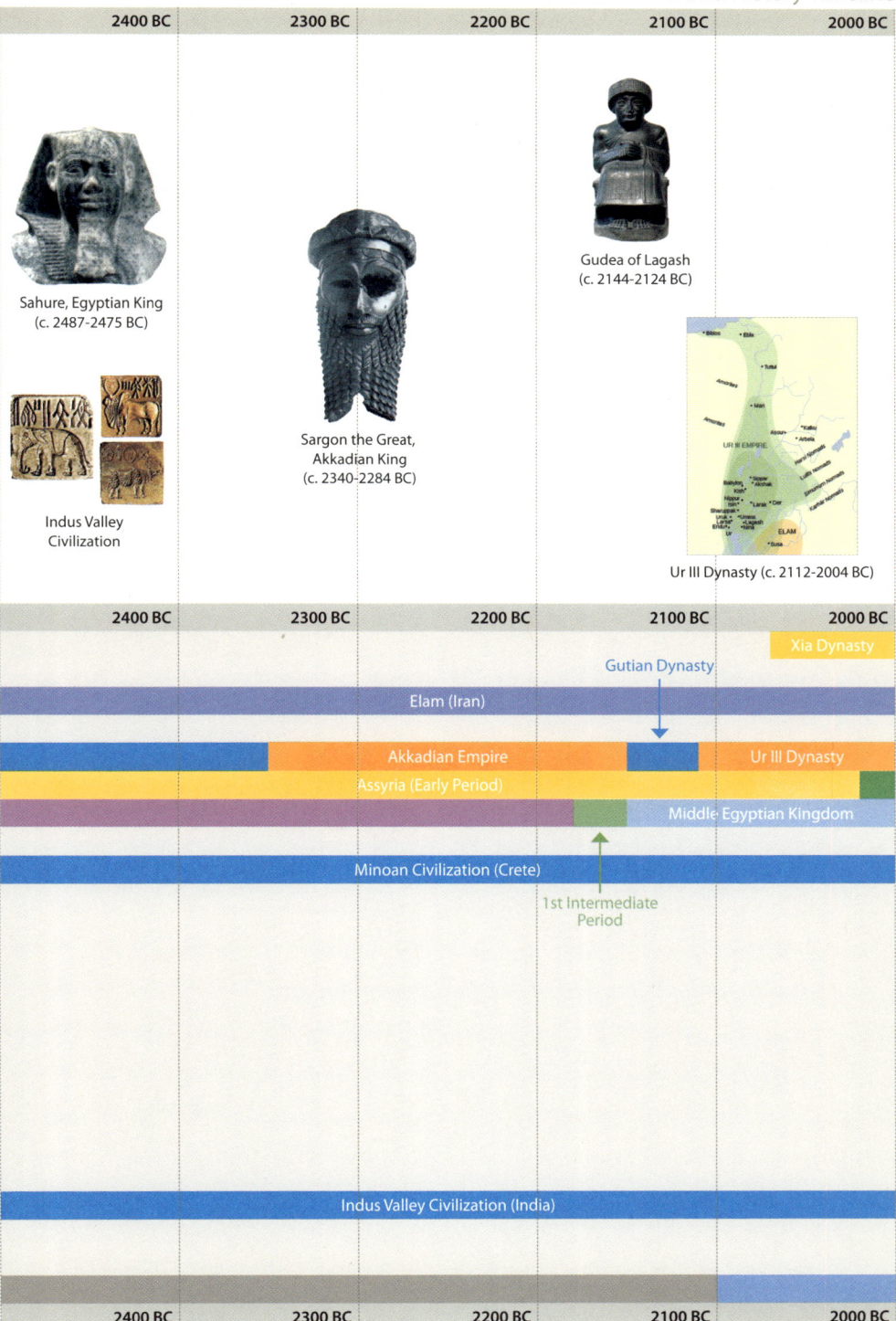

| 2400 BC | 2300 BC | 2200 BC | 2100 BC | 2000 BC |

Sahure, Egyptian King
(c. 2487-2475 BC)

Indus Valley
Civilization

Sargon the Great,
Akkadian King
(c. 2340-2284 BC)

Gudea of Lagash
(c. 2144-2124 BC)

Ur III Dynasty (c. 2112-2004 BC)

| 2400 BC | 2300 BC | 2200 BC | 2100 BC | 2000 BC |

Xia Dynasty

Gutian Dynasty

Elam (Iran)

Akkadian Empire

Ur III Dynasty

Assyria (Early Period)

Middle Egyptian Kingdom

Minoan Civilization (Crete)

1st Intermediate
Period

Indus Valley Civilization (India)

| 2400 BC | 2300 BC | 2200 BC | 2100 BC | 2000 BC |

World History Timeline

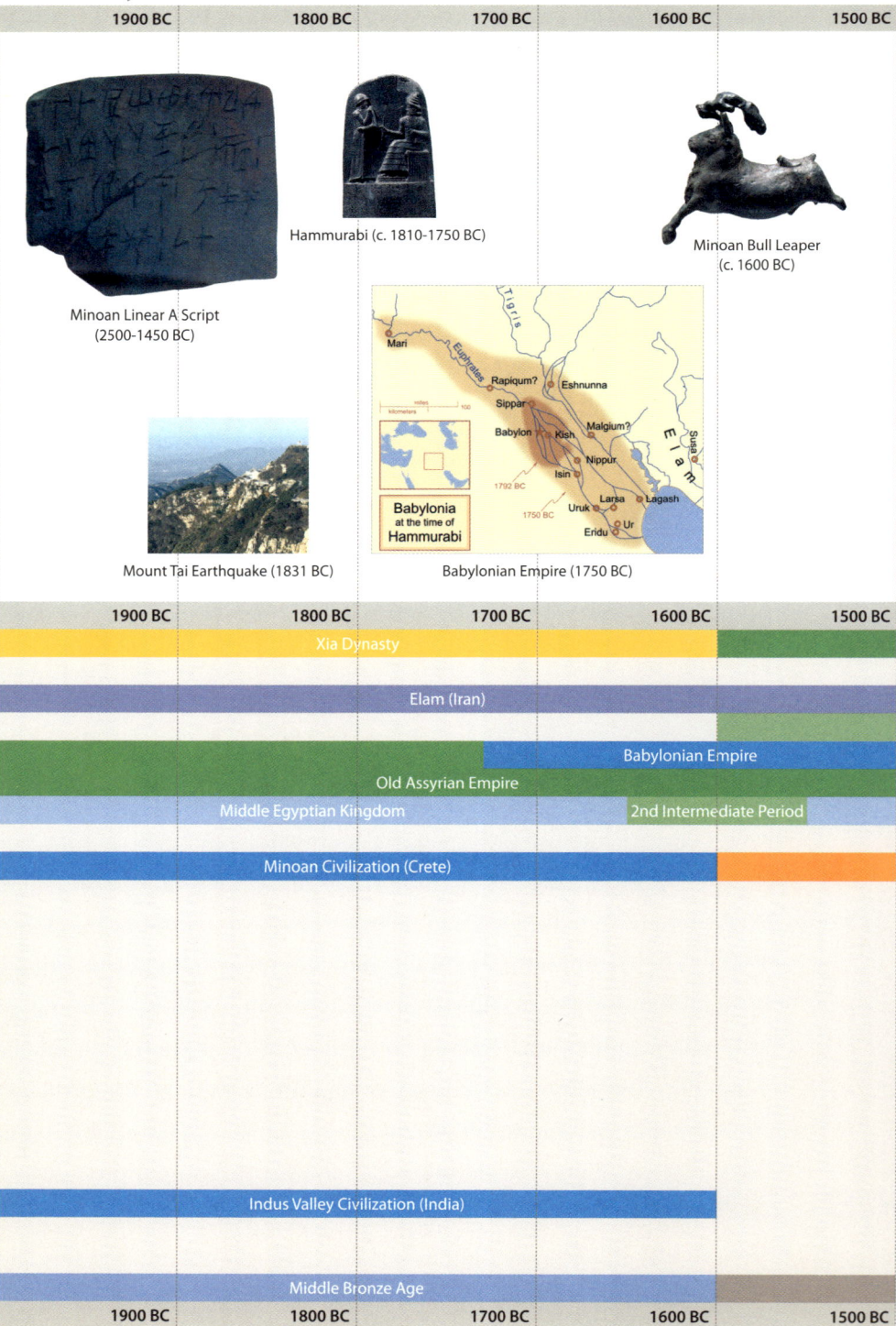

1900 BC	1800 BC	1700 BC	1600 BC	1500 BC

Minoan Linear A Script
(2500-1450 BC)

Hammurabi (c. 1810-1750 BC)

Minoan Bull Leaper
(c. 1600 BC)

Mount Tai Earthquake (1831 BC)

Babylonia
at the time of
Hammurabi

Babylonian Empire (1750 BC)

1900 BC	1800 BC	1700 BC	1600 BC	1500 BC

Xia Dynasty

Elam (Iran)

Babylonian Empire

Old Assyrian Empire

Middle Egyptian Kingdom

2nd Intermediate Period

Minoan Civilization (Crete)

Indus Valley Civilization (India)

Middle Bronze Age

1900 BC	1800 BC	1700 BC	1600 BC	1500 BC

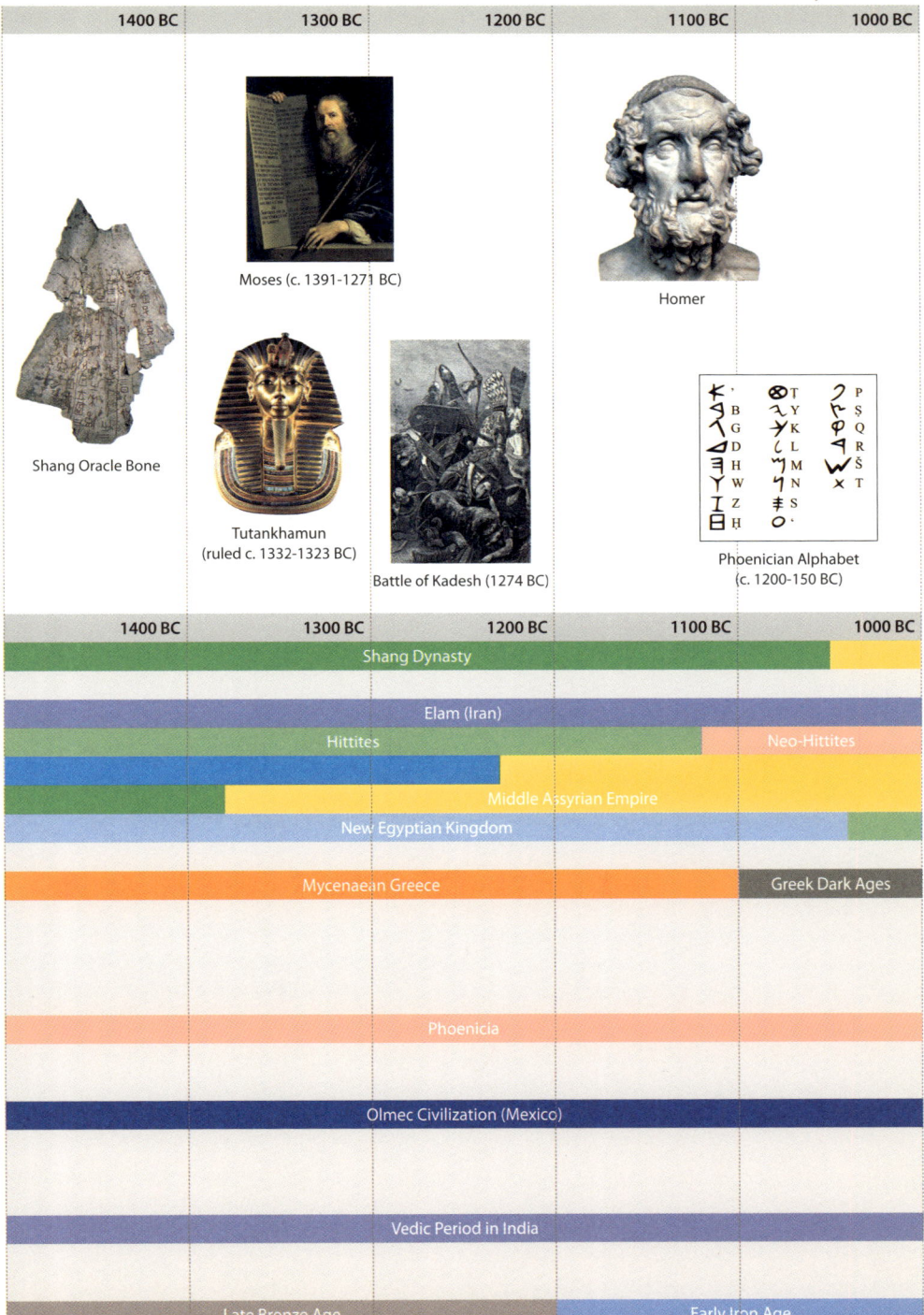

| 1400 BC | 1300 BC | 1200 BC | 1100 BC | 1000 BC |

Moses (c. 1391-1271 BC)

Homer

Shang Oracle Bone

Tutankhamun
(ruled c. 1332-1323 BC)

Battle of Kadesh (1274 BC)

Phoenician Alphabet
(c. 1200-150 BC)

| 1400 BC | 1300 BC | 1200 BC | 1100 BC | 1000 BC |

Shang Dynasty

Elam (Iran)

Hittites

Neo-Hittites

Middle Assyrian Empire

New Egyptian Kingdom

Mycenaean Greece

Greek Dark Ages

Phoenicia

Olmec Civilization (Mexico)

Vedic Period in India

Late Bronze Age

Early Iron Age

| 1400 BC | 1300 BC | 1200 BC | 1100 BC | 1000 BC |

World History Timeline

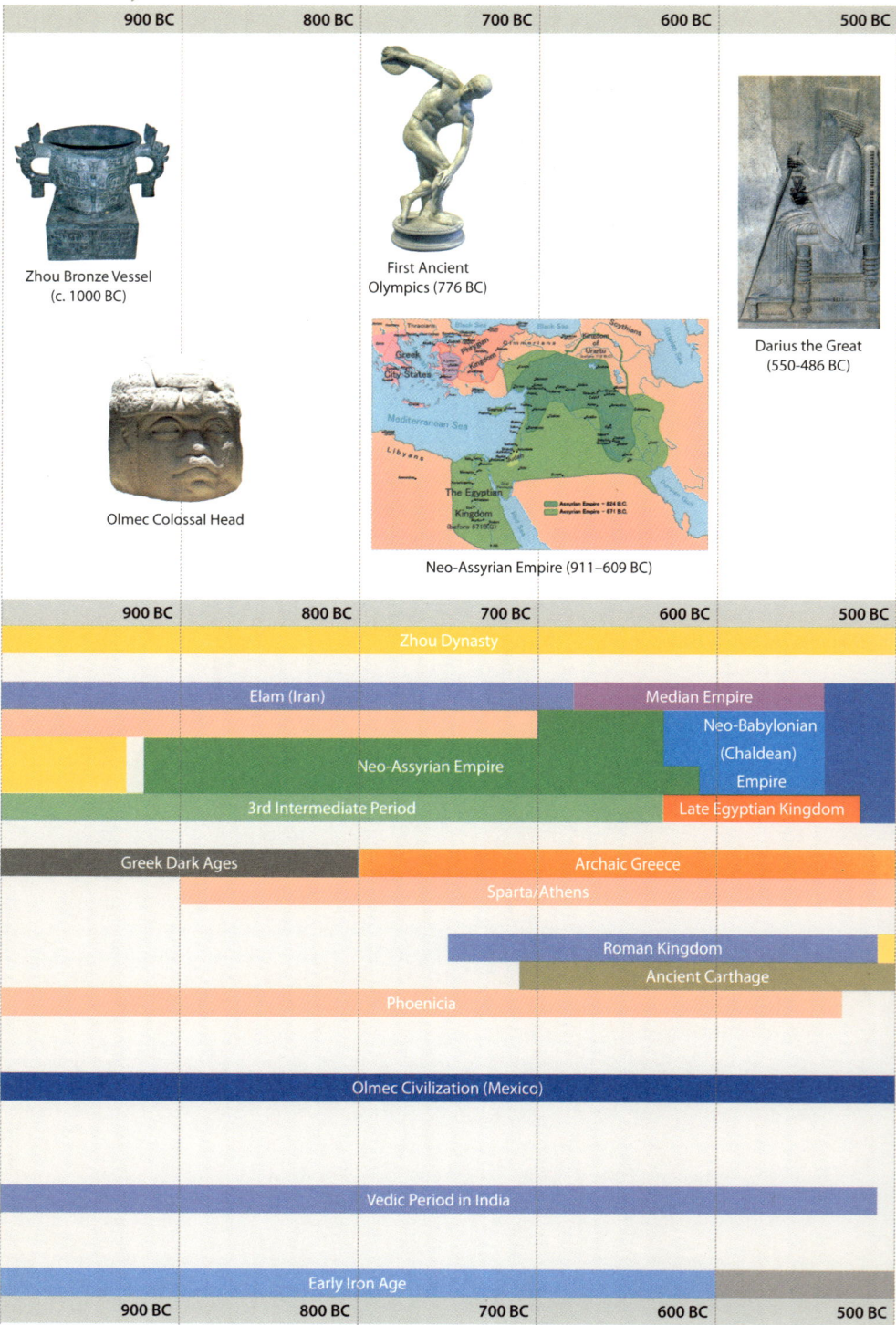

| | 900 BC | 800 BC | 700 BC | 600 BC | 500 BC |

Zhou Bronze Vessel
(c. 1000 BC)

First Ancient
Olympics (776 BC)

Darius the Great
(550-486 BC)

Olmec Colossal Head

Neo-Assyrian Empire (911–609 BC)

| | 900 BC | 800 BC | 700 BC | 600 BC | 500 BC |

Zhou Dynasty

Elam (Iran)

Median Empire

Neo-Babylonian
(Chaldean)
Empire

Neo-Assyrian Empire

3rd Intermediate Period

Late Egyptian Kingdom

Greek Dark Ages

Archaic Greece

Sparta/Athens

Roman Kingdom

Ancient Carthage

Phoenicia

Olmec Civilization (Mexico)

Vedic Period in India

Early Iron Age

| | 900 BC | 800 BC | 700 BC | 600 BC | 500 BC |

World History Timeline

| 400 BC | 300 BC | 200 BC | 100 BC | 0 |

Alexander the Great
(356-323 BC)

Julius Caesar
(100-44 BC)

Cleopatra
(69-30 BC)

Battle of Salamis
(480 BC)

Hannibal
(247-183 BC)

Rossetta Stone
(created 196 BC)

Seleucid Empire (312-63 BC)

| 400 BC | 300 BC | 200 BC | 100 BC | 0 |

Zhou Dynasty

Qin

Han Dynasty

Achaemenid (Persian) Empire

Alexander the Great

Parthian Empire

Seleucid Empire
Ptolemaic Kingdom
(Hellenistic Greece)

Classical Greece

Roman Empire

Sparta/Athens

Roman Republic

Roman Empire

Maurya Empire

Middle Iron Age

| 400 BC | 300 BC | 200 BC | 100 BC | 0 |

World History Timeline

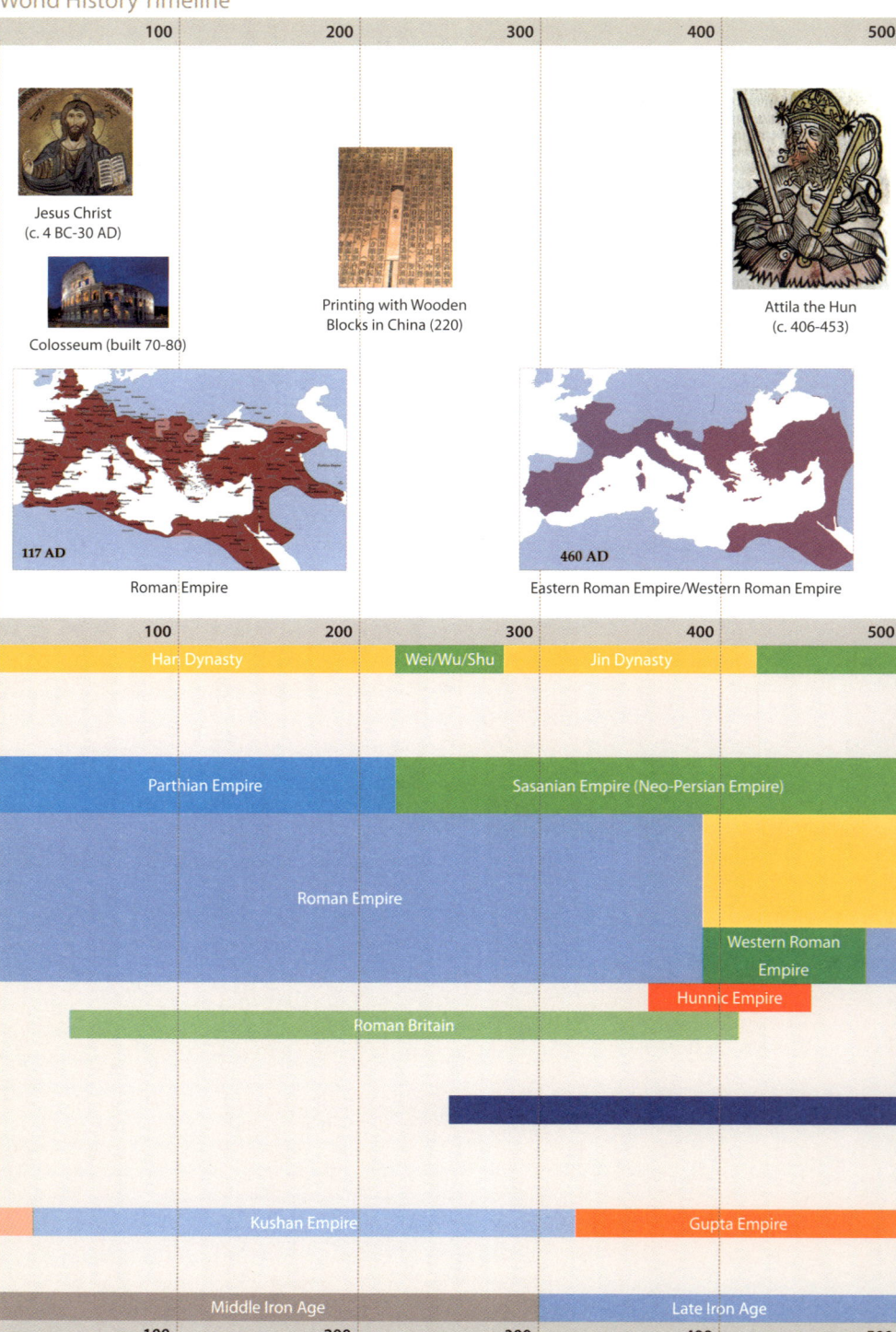

	100	200	300	400	500

Jesus Christ
(c. 4 BC–30 AD)

Colosseum (built 70–80)

Printing with Wooden
Blocks in China (220)

Attila the Hun
(c. 406–453)

117 AD

Roman Empire

460 AD

Eastern Roman Empire/Western Roman Empire

	100	200	300	400	500

Han Dynasty

Wei/Wu/Shu

Jin Dynasty

Parthian Empire

Sasanian Empire (Neo-Persian Empire)

Roman Empire

Western Roman Empire

Hunnic Empire

Roman Britain

Kushan Empire

Gupta Empire

Middle Iron Age

Late Iron Age

	100	200	300	400	500

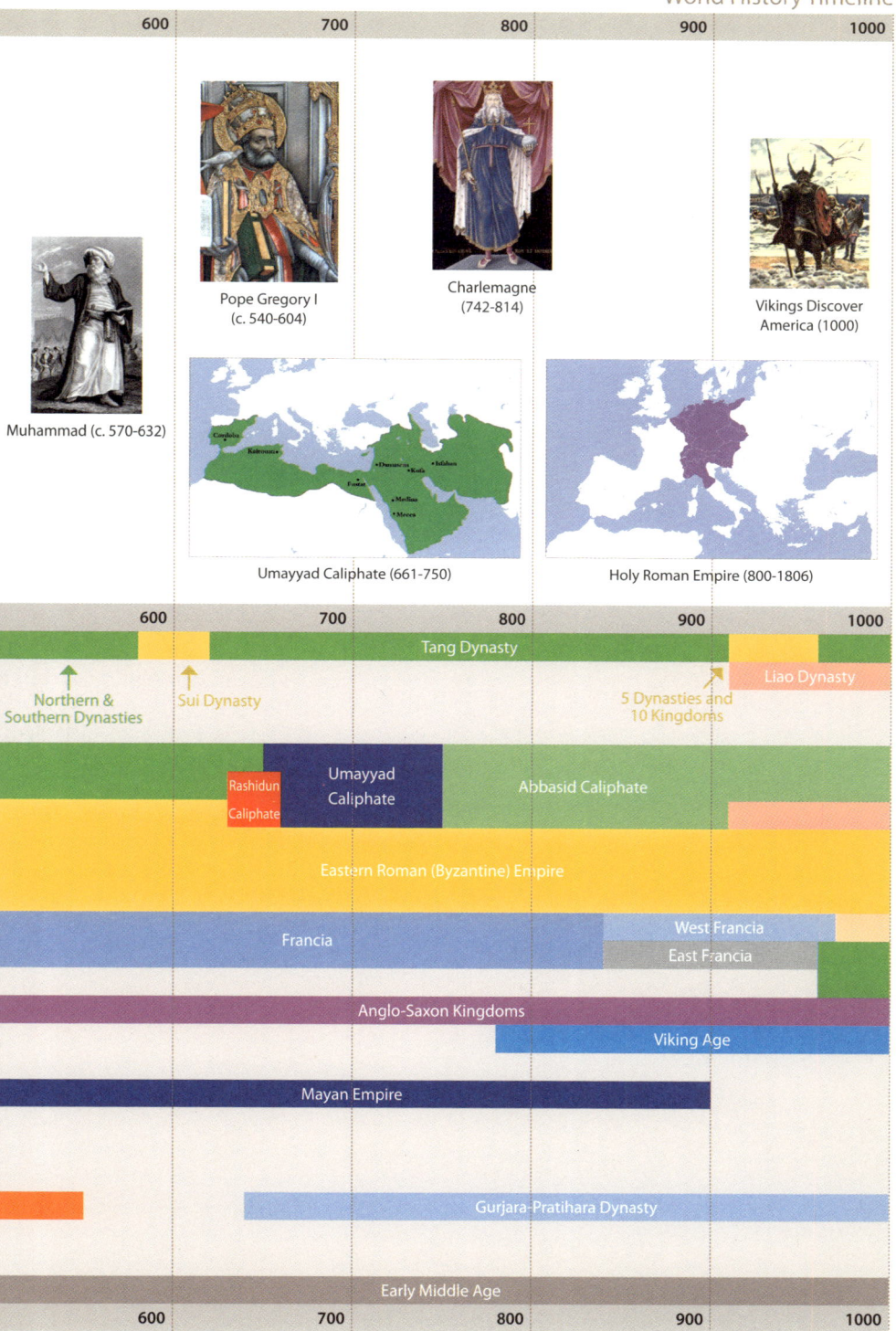

600   700   800   900   1000

Pope Gregory I
(c. 540-604)

Charlemagne
(742-814)

Vikings Discover
America (1000)

Muhammad (c. 570-632)

Umayyad Caliphate (661-750)

Holy Roman Empire (800-1806)

600   700   800   900   1000

Tang Dynasty

Liao Dynasty

Northern &
Southern Dynasties

Sui Dynasty

5 Dynasties and
10 Kingdoms

Rashidun
Caliphate

Umayyad
Caliphate

Abbasid Caliphate

Eastern Roman (Byzantine) Empire

Francia

West Francia

East Francia

Anglo-Saxon Kingdoms

Viking Age

Mayan Empire

Gurjara-Pratihara Dynasty

Early Middle Age

600   700   800   900   1000

World History Timeline

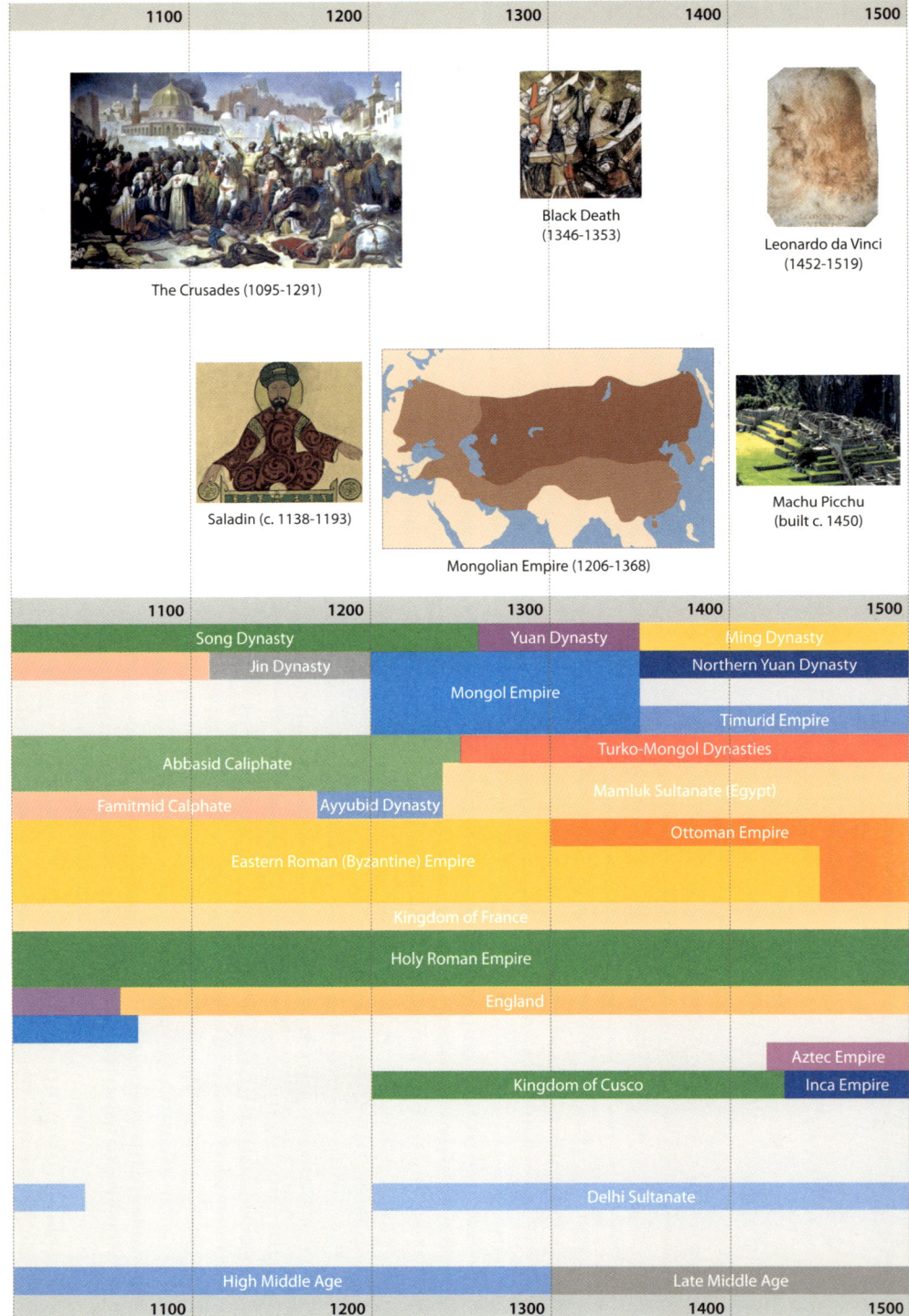

The Crusades (1095-1291)

Black Death (1346-1353)

Leonardo da Vinci (1452-1519)

Saladin (c. 1138-1193)

Mongolian Empire (1206-1368)

Machu Picchu (built c. 1450)

| 1100 | 1200 | 1300 | 1400 | 1500 |

Song Dynasty
Yuan Dynasty
Ming Dynasty
Jin Dynasty
Northern Yuan Dynasty
Mongol Empire
Timurid Empire
Abbasid Caliphate
Turko-Mongol Dynasties
Famitmid Calphate
Ayyubid Dynasty
Mamluk Sultanate (Egypt)
Ottoman Empire
Eastern Roman (Byzantine) Empire
Kingdom of France
Holy Roman Empire
England
Aztec Empire
Inca Empire
Kingdom of Cusco
Delhi Sultanate
High Middle Age
Late Middle Age

| 1100 | 1200 | 1300 | 1400 | 1500 |

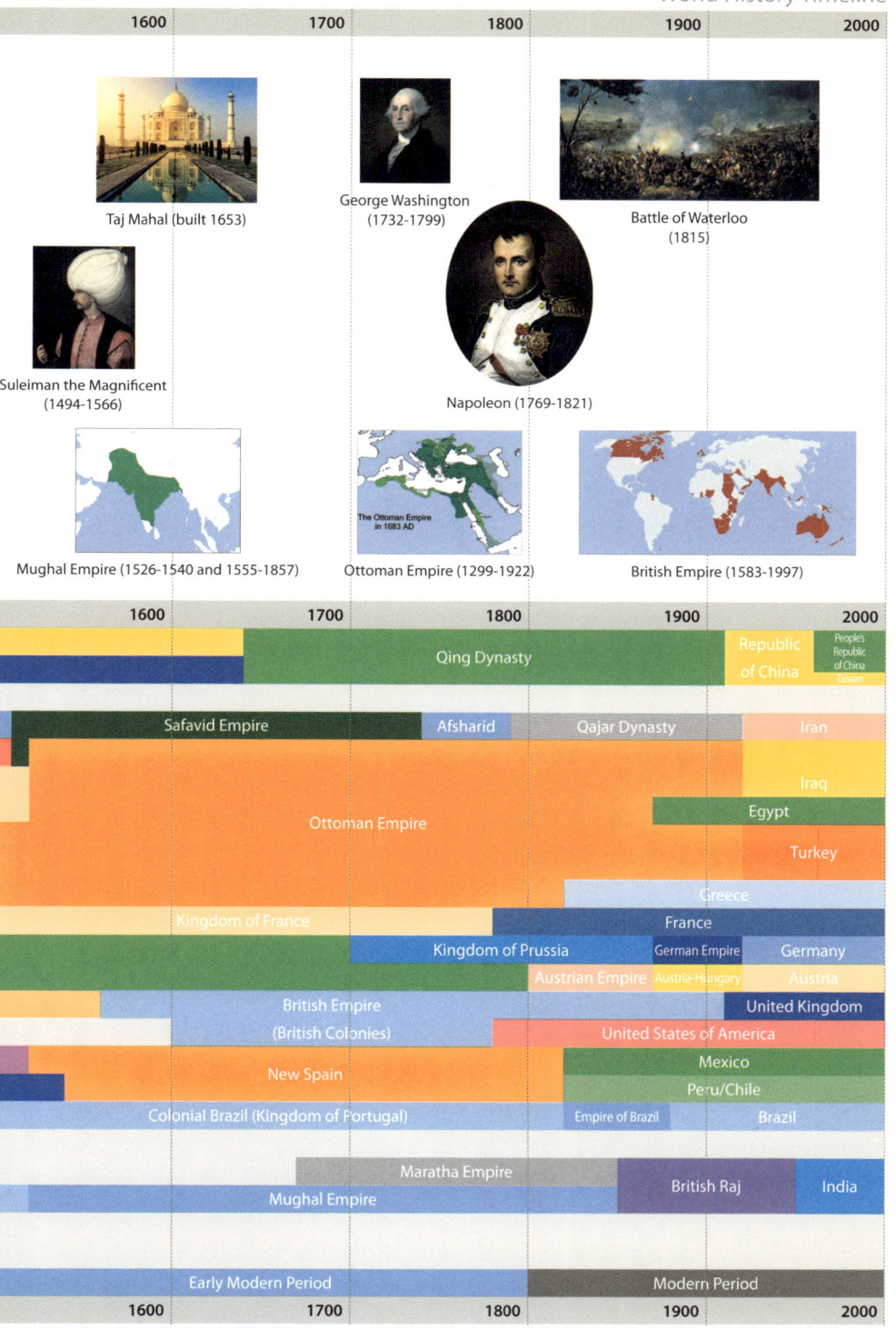

World History Timeline

Taj Mahal (built 1653)

George Washington (1732-1799)

Battle of Waterloo (1815)

Suleiman the Magnificent (1494-1566)

Napoleon (1769-1821)

Mughal Empire (1526-1540 and 1555-1857)

The Ottoman Empire in 1683 AD

Ottoman Empire (1299-1922)

British Empire (1583-1997)

Qing Dynasty — Republic of China — People's Republic of China / Taiwan

Safavid Empire — Afsharid — Qajar Dynasty — Iran

Ottoman Empire — Iraq — Egypt — Turkey — Greece

Kingdom of France — France

Kingdom of Prussia — German Empire — Germany

Austrian Empire — Austria-Hungary — Austria

British Empire (British Colonies) — United Kingdom

United States of America

New Spain — Mexico — Peru/Chile

Colonial Brazil (Kingdom of Portugal) — Empire of Brazil — Brazil

Maratha Empire — British Raj — India

Mughal Empire

Early Modern Period — Modern Period

List of Books